The Lady of Shalott

ALFRED, LORD TENNYSON

The Lady *of* Shalott

WITH ILLUSTRATIONS BY

GENEVIÈVE CÔTÉ

KCP POETRY

An Imprint of Kids Can Press

PART I

*O*n either side the river lie
Long fields of barley and of rye,
That clothe the wold and meet the sky;
And thro' the field the road runs by
　　To many-tower'd Camelot;
And up and down the people go,
Gazing where the lilies blow
Round an island there below,
　　The island of Shalott.

Willows whiten, aspens quiver,
Little breezes dusk and shiver
Thro' the wave that runs for ever
By the island in the river
    Flowing down to Camelot.
Four gray walls, and four gray towers,
Overlook a space of flowers,
And the silent isle imbowers
    The Lady of Shalott.

By the margin, willow-veil'd,
Slide the heavy barges trail'd
By slow horses; and unhail'd
The shallop flitteth silken-sail'd
     Skimming down to Camelot:
But who hath seen her wave her hand?
Or at the casement seen her stand?
Or is she known in all the land,
     The Lady of Shalott?

*O*nly reapers, reaping early
In among the bearded barley,
Hear a song that echoes cheerly
From the river winding clearly,
    Down to tower'd Camelot;
And by the moon the reaper weary,
Piling sheaves in uplands airy,
Listening, whispers "'Tis the fairy
    Lady of Shalott."

PART II

There she weaves by night and day
A magic web with colours gay.
She has heard a whisper say,
A curse is on her if she stay
　　To look down to Camelot.
She knows not what the curse may be,
And so she weaveth steadily,
And little other care hath she,
　　The Lady of Shalott.

And moving thro' a mirror clear
That hangs before her all the year,
Shadows of the world appear.
There she sees the highway near
  Winding down to Camelot;
There the river eddy whirls,
And there the surly village-churls,
And the red cloaks of market girls,
  Pass onward from Shalott.

Sometimes a troop of damsels glad,
An abbot on an ambling pad,
Sometimes a curly shepherd-lad,
Or long-hair'd page in crimson clad,
    Goes by to tower'd Camelot;

And sometimes thro' the mirror blue
The knights come riding two and two:
She hath no loyal knight and true,
    The Lady of Shalott.

*B*ut in her web she still delights
To weave the mirror's magic sights,
For often thro' the silent nights
A funeral, with plumes and lights
    And music, went to Camelot;
Or when the moon was overhead,
Came two young lovers lately wed:

"*I* am half sick of shadows," said
The Lady of Shalott.

PART III

A bow-shot from her bower-eaves,
He rode between the barley-sheaves,
The sun came dazzling thro' the leaves,
And flamed upon the brazen greaves
        Of bold Sir Lancelot.
A red-cross knight for ever kneel'd
To a lady in his shield,
That sparkled on the yellow field,
        Beside remote Shalott.

The gemmy bridle glitter'd free,
Like to some branch of stars we see
Hung in the golden Galaxy.
The bridle bells rang merrily
        As he rode down to Camelot;
And from his blazon'd baldric slung
A mighty silver bugle hung,
And as he rode his armour rung,
        Beside remote Shalott.

All in the blue unclouded weather
Thick-jewell'd shone the saddle-leather,
The helmet and the helmet-feather
Burn'd like one burning flame together,
     As he rode down to Camelot;
As often thro' the purple night,
Below the starry clusters bright,
Some bearded meteor, trailing light,
     Moves over still Shalott.

$\mathcal{H}$is broad clear brow in sunlight glow'd;
On burnish'd hooves his war-horse trode;
From underneath his helmet flow'd
His coal-black curls as on he rode,
    As he rode down to Camelot.
From the bank and from the river
He flash'd into the crystal mirror,
"Tirra lirra," by the river
    Sang Sir Lancelot.

She left the web, she left the loom,
She made three paces thro' the room,
She saw the water-lily bloom,
She saw the helmet and the plume,
　　She look'd down to Camelot.
Out flew the web and floated wide;
The mirror crack'd from side to side;
"The curse is come upon me," cried
　　The Lady of Shalott.

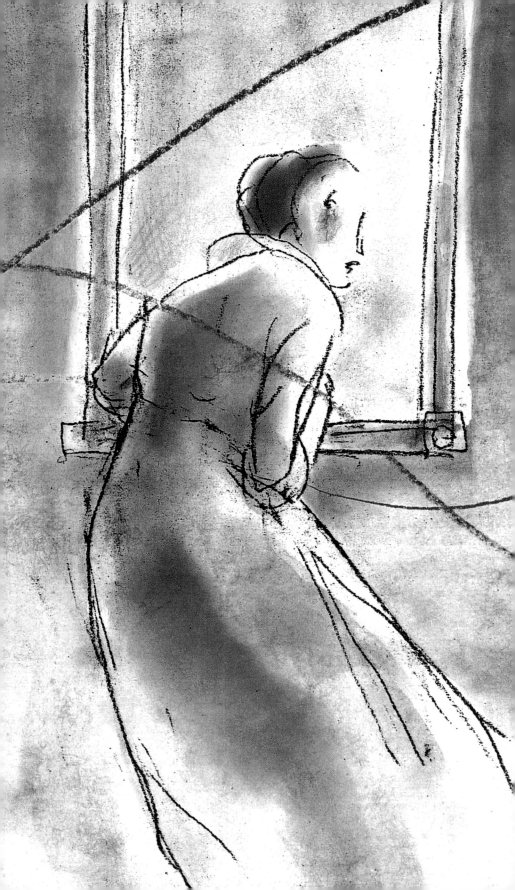

PART IV

*I*n the stormy east-wind straining,
The pale yellow woods were waning,
The broad stream in his banks complaining,
Heavily the low sky raining
      Over tower'd Camelot;
Down she came and found a boat
Beneath a willow left afloat,
And round about the prow she wrote
      The Lady of Shalott.

*A*nd down the river's dim expanse
Like some bold seer in a trance,
Seeing all his own mischance —
With a glassy countenance
        Did she look to Camelot.
And at the closing of the day
She loosed the chain, and down she lay;
The broad stream bore her far away,
        The Lady of Shalott.

*L*ying, robed in snowy white
That loosely flew to left and right —
The leaves upon her falling light —
Thro' the noises of the night
  She floated down to Camelot;
And as the boat-head wound along
The willowy hills and fields among,
They heard her singing her last song,
  The Lady of Shalott.

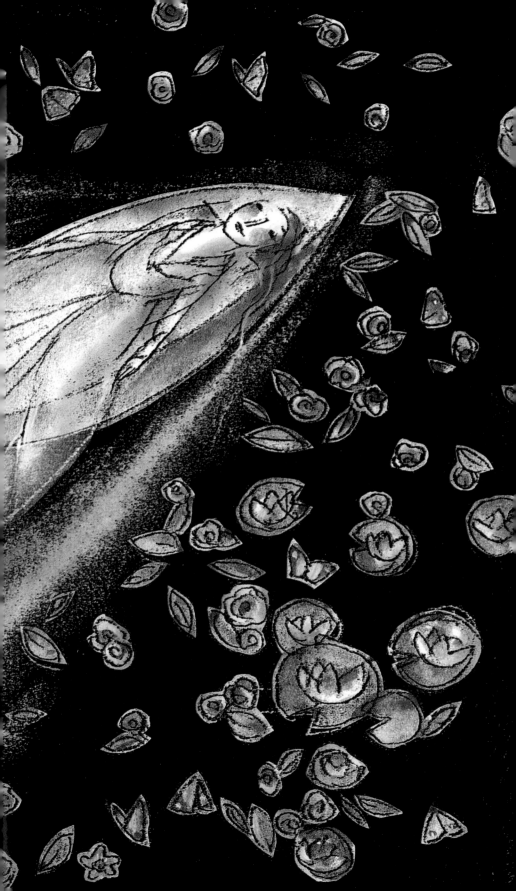

Heard a carol, mournful, holy,
Chanted loudly, chanted lowly,
Till her blood was frozen slowly,
And her eyes were darken'd wholly,
　　Turn'd to tower'd Camelot.
For ere she reach'd upon the tide
The first house by the water-side,
Singing in her song she died,
　　The Lady of Shalott.

Under tower and balcony,
By garden-wall and gallery,
A gleaming shape she floated by,
Dead-pale between the houses high,
    Silent into Camelot.
Out upon the wharfs they came,
Knight and burgher, lord and dame,
And round the prow they read her name,
    The Lady of Shalott.

*W*ho is this? and what is here?
And in the lighted palace near
Died the sound of royal cheer;
And they cross'd themselves for fear,
　　All the knights at Camelot:
But Lancelot mused a little space;
He said, "She has a lovely face;
God in his mercy lend her grace,
　　The Lady of Shalott."

Alfred, Lord Tennyson

The most famous poet of the Victorian age, Alfred Tennyson (1809–92) is also regarded as one of the preeminent English poets of all time. Tennyson possessed a marvelous ability to craft evocative imagery and to use landscapes to convey emotion. Even his harshest critics have recognized his gift for lyric poetry, which is arguably unequaled in the history of English verse. Queen Victoria appointed Tennyson, a greatly esteemed spokesman for the ideas and values of the era, Poet Laureate in 1850.

Although written over a century ago, his poems, such as "Ulysses," "The Lotos-Eaters," *In Memoriam* and "The Charge of the Light Brigade," have maintained their popularity. So, too, has the beloved "The Lady of Shalott." This romantic narrative of unrequited love set in Arthurian England reflects Tennyson's obsession with the past, particularly his lifelong fascination with King Arthur and his court, and conjures the magic of this fabled time. Originally published in 1832, then much revised for his 1842 edition of *Poems*, its lyrical language and masterful meter make for some of the most memorable lines in English poetry.

The rich symbolism of "The Lady of Shalott" has invited diverse interpretations: It has been understood as a commentary on the role of women in the Victorian period, who, much like the poem's imprisoned maiden, were relegated to the private sphere of the home and separated from the public sphere of men; and as an exploration of the relationship of the artist to society — the Lady, isolated from the world with her endless weaving, being a metaphor for the artist. Others have perceived it as a reflection on nature versus industry or as a meditation on the passage toward death.

It is a fitting tribute to Tennyson's literary genius that "The Lady of Shalott," considered one of the most beautiful, mysterious and haunting poems in the English language, is as mesmerizing to us today as it was to those of yesteryear.

Geneviève Côté

The inspiration for many famous paintings, "The Lady of Shalott" has enthralled artists since the Victorian era. Illustrator Geneviève Côté is one who has fallen under the spell of this poem, drawn by its universal themes of love and death and its ideas about women and art. Her vision of Tennyson's poem, however, stands apart from earlier depictions, particularly the theatrically ornate creations of Pre-Raphaelite artists such as John William Waterhouse and William Holman Hunt. The timelessness and delicate minimalism of Côté's images, reminiscent of the elegant, simplified forms and flowing lines of Modigliani, result in a refreshingly modern rendering of a classic regularly depicted in an Arthurian setting. Her sensitive interpretation also weaves an unexpectedly hopeful twist into what has generally been perceived as a tragic poem about a woman's journey toward death. Côté fashions a brilliant visual metaphor of the Lady as a chrysalis-like figure who metamorphoses into a beautiful butterfly upon breaking free from the confining cocoon of her tower.

With her ethereal illustrations, Côté has truly captured the magical and mystical spirit of this captivating poem, especially that of the enigmatic "fairy Lady" herself. Yet using the exquisite threads spun by Tennyson, she has woven a luminous tapestry of her own — one that will enchant readers of all ages.

Geneviève Côté has illustrated several picture books and early novels for children, including *The Amazing Story of the Little Black Sheep* and *Minn and Jake*. Her editorial art has appeared in such publications as the *New York Times*, the *Boston Globe* and the *Wall Street Journal*. Throughout her career, Côté has received many honors, among them a Silver Award from the New York Society of Illustrators and two nominations for the Governor General's Award for Illustration, Canada's highest literary prize. She lives in Montreal, Quebec.

To Marie C.
And many thanks to all those who have
immortalized the Lady of Shalott by sharing
their love of this extraordinary poem through
their own writing and works of art — G.C.

╫

The illustrations for this book were rendered in mixed media.

The text was set in
Celeste and *Dorchester Script*

╫

KCP Poetry is an imprint of Kids Can Press

Illustrations © 2005 Geneviève Côté

Kids Can Press acknowledges the financial support of the Government of
Ontario, through the Ontario Media Development Corporation's Ontario Book
Initiative; the Ontario Arts Council; the Canada Council for the Arts; and
the Government of Canada, through the BPIDP, for our publishing activity.

Published in Canada by   Published in the U.S. by
Kids Can Press Ltd.   Kids Can Press Ltd.
29 Birch Avenue   2250 Military Road
Toronto, ON M4V 1E2   Tonawanda, NY 14150

www.kidscanpress.com

Edited by Tara Walker
Designed by Karen Powers
Printed and bound in China

This book is smyth sewn casebound.

CM 05 0 9 8 7 6 5 4 3 2 1

Library and Archives Canada Cataloguing in Publication

Tennyson, Alfred Tennyson, Baron, 1809–1892.
The lady of Shalott / Alfred, Lord Tennyson ;
with illustrations by Geneviève Côté.

(Visions in poetry)

ISBN 1-55337-874-1

1. Children's poetry, English. I. Côté, Geneviève
II. Title. III. Series.

PR5563.L33 2005   j821'.8   C2004-907371-0

Kids Can Press is a ℓ☺ℾUsᵀᴹ Entertainment company